THE
BROCHURE
STRATEGY

**A UNIQUE APPROACH TO A SUCCESSFUL CAREER
CHANGE THAT WILL OPEN UNREALIZED
DOORS OF OPPORTUNITY**

BRUCE R. MATZA

THE
BROCHURE
STRATEGY

ABOUT THE AUTHOR

Bruce R. Matza brings a wealth of experience in strategic planning, staff & customer retention, and customer service. He has experience with such prominent brands as Neiman Marcus, where he was a senior executive for 20 years.

He has advised numerous organizations including Walt Disney World, Harrods of London, Marriott, Motorola, Michigan and Minnesota Funeral Directors Associations, Texas Association of REALTORS®, National Retail Federation, National Restaurant Association, California & Minnesota Society of Association Executives, US Chamber of Commerce, United Way Worldwide and many others.

He is author and creator of *Becoming a Customer Service Star*, initially designed for Walt Disney World. It is in a 3rd edition published by HRDQ and to date has sold over 250,000 copies to organizations interested in the enhancement of their customer satisfaction initiatives.

Bruce served honorably as an officer in the U.S. Air force and has been featured in many articles and stories in addition to appearing on The NBC Today Show.

ANOTHER PUBLICATION
BY BRUCE R. MATZA

Becoming a Customer Service STAR

Published by HRDQ   www.HRDQ.com

A learning instrument that provides a personal inventory of your Customer Service aptitude. *Becoming a Customer Service STAR* will help you and your people achieve your customer service goals.

Whether you work with customers face-to-face, by phone, or via the internet, this tool will boost the development of five skills that are critical to your success.

△   Maintain a positive attitude

△   Encourage customer feedback

△   Respond effectively to customer issues

△   Develop relationships with your customers

△   Exceed customer expectations

Over 250,000 copies have been sold.

QUOTES FROM SUCCESSFUL
BROCHURE STRATEGY EXPERIENCES

"Simple networking concept that is innovative and amazingly effective. The Brochure Strategy will get you in front of decision-makers who will become your best advocate!"

"Brochure Strategy will open unrealized doors of opportunity."

"Brochure Strategy puts reinventing oneself into motion!"

"Brochure Strategy is practical and will get you results!"

"Following the step-by-step approach of the Brochure Strategy will by-pass any self-defeating doubts and paralysis to assure you take action."

TABLE OF CONTENTS

DEDICATION

Bitty, for fifty years you have been my loyal and loving spouse and dedicated partner. You have supported me through more than our share of career changes.

I love you. Our life together would fill many brochures.

INTRODUCTION

You are about to learn a unique networking approach to a successful career change by building referrals and getting in front of decision-makers. The Brochure Strategy is for anyone in a position of leadership looking for a new career direction.

Here is a proven job search process for managers and executives that does not depend on resumes and cover letters. It can lead to new employment opportunities as well as open doors to becoming a consulting adviser and specialist.

The brochure also helps you formulate your value to a prospective company that serves you well from both a consulting and employment point of view.

The Brochure Strategy is a proactive, self-motivating process that allows you to present all your skills, qualities, and values to a prospective company. You will be in total in control of your future career search.

Chapter 1

THE SITUATION

You have been downsized, laid off, or early retired. With years of work experience, you are back in the job market competing with people half your age and dealing with impersonal electronic on-line applications.

You wrestle with the thought of having to write a resume and a strong cover letter. Just the thought of having to send out hundreds of resumes is exhausting.

If you get an interview it is with someone who is half your age, in Human Resources with a fraction of your experience who is more likely to judge you based on the college from which you graduated than the jobs that you have held.

The entire experience is demoralizing and depressing. You wish there was a more appropriate way to get in front of decision makers without having to play the resume, cover letter and on-line application game.

How do you avoid the resume cover letter game

Enter the Brochure Strategy.

Chapter 2

MY PERSONAL EXPERIENCE

I departed corporate life in 1990 and was advised by a friend to design a brochure to better define my next career move. The center of the brochure described three major areas of expertise including my experience in customer service programs. When I thought about who could provide a testimonial for the back panel, I remembered an executive of a major Fortune 500 company who was very complimentary of several programs I conducted for his staff as a guest speaker.

I called Richard and asked if I could use a quote and he graciously provided an incredibly positive statement and asked me to send him several copies of the brochure. The brochure was a draft for my personal use and suddenly I had to print half a dozen copies. A week later, I got a call from Richard indicating he received my brochure and was surprised to see that one of my consulting areas was Customer Service. It seems his organization was looking for someone to design and conduct customer service training for employees in twenty facilities around the country.

I was able to visit his headquarters, meet with staff and executives and learn what they had done in the past. I drafted a proposal that included proposed curriculum, defined outcomes, schedule of training sessions, costs and expenses. I had no idea how to price my services, so I called Richard and asked what they paid other consultants. I priced my services based on information he shared with me. My proposal was accepted and provided my first client worth over $100,000.

Chapter 3

A BRIEF BACKGROUND

Years ago, when I left corporate life, there were dozens of managers and executives that followed me out the doors in the years that followed. Each would call and ask if I could help write a resume, make some interview introductions, and network them back into the job market.

Since job hunting is nothing but a mathematical process:

Some number of resumes and cover letters will get you in front of an HR representative.

A smaller number will get you a call-back interview.

Far fewer will result in you having the opportunity to be sitting in front of a decision maker.

I know this mathematical process is exhausting and depressing and continually have tried to find ways to help people reduce the odds.

Thus, the Brochure Strategy was born.

Chapter 4

THE TYPICAL RESUME APPROACH

Often you will start calling friends, neighbors and past business contacts to begin the networking process and maybe secure a possible interview. When you call someone about a job interview, they think about what they know you did in the past or they look on your resume. That gets them to focus on one skill or activity and you must spend much of your time and energy to get them to see you in a broader capacity.

If they don't know someone to refer you to, and have no immediate job opportunity to discuss with you, they give you the standard response, "Send me a copy of your resume and I will keep it on file if something comes up."

This is the kiss of death. Your resume either sits on someone's desk or gets put into the HR files. Either way it has a shelf life of about two days to a week.

"Send me a copy of your resume," is the kiss of death!

If you apply to a larger company your basic qualifications are keyed into a computer program and you get a call if the skills they need match something specific on your

resume. Congratulations, your fate rests with the latest human resources software program.

Chapter 5

RESUMES ARE
A MATHEMATICAL GAME

The other alternative is sending out copies of your resume and a cover letter in hopes of getting an interview. This is a total mathematical game. Somewhere amongst the 250 to 500 resumes you circulate, there are a couple of possible job interviews, but this process is demoralizing and ineffective.

Here is why resumes and cover letters are a mathematical game.

→   You are going to send out 250 to 500 Resumes and Cover Letters.

→   You will attempt to follow-up with 75 to 150 phone calls.

→   You may be lucky to get 15 to 25 First Interviews.

→   That might result in 7 to 10 Call-back Interviews.

→   Your chances are good to be invited to 4 or 5 Decision Level Interviews.

➔ You may potentially receive 1 or 2 Job Offers.

➔ You will finally accept a job based on the position, the money or just the desire to end the search process.

The key to a successful search is to begin the process as high on the Mathematics chart as possible.

This process is exhausting, demoralizing and keeps you in a defensive posture. When you finally get an interview, you are lucky to be able to introduce two or three specific accomplishments into the discussion because you don't even control the flow of the conversation.

The person conducting the interview asks the questions, presses you for specifics and moves on to the next set of questions. You are lucky to be able to share just a few of your accomplishments and qualifications.

You are totally on the defensive, even if you find a way to begin the search process farther up the mathematical game chart.

I have friends who distributed resumes and cover letters for months. They got up each morning and worked diligently to identify 5 to 10 businesses and organizations that had online job listings. Each would get a resume and personalized cover letter.

These folks would struggle to follow-up with phone calls to assure the resume and letter were received and try to get an initial interview.

Most considered this a successful job search and knew little else to do but continue the process day after day.

A successful job search should not require the exhausting exercise of sending resumes, cover letters and follow-up calls for an interview.

Chapter 6

AN ENTIRELY DIFFERENT APPROACH

Consider for a moment that you do not approach people for a job interview, but instead indicate that you are considering the possibility of starting your own consulting business and would appreciate their advice. You have designed an initial brochure that shows the areas you have a level of expertise to become a consultant for them to review. You would like to meet for coffee and get their suggestions.

"I am thinking about starting my own business.

I have some rough ideas but would value your advice.

Can we meet for coffee?"

The brochure strategy works in an entirely different way because it you get in front of decision-makers and they see the all of your abilities.

You no longer send out resumes, make follow-up calls or try to find someone willing to give you a job interview. You are going to promote the idea of going into business for yourself. Now do not get defensive, this strategy is

just to get in front of decision makers. There is a chance the Brochure Strategy leads you to a self-employed opportunity, but it is as likely to open doors for full-time employment.

The process is motivating because each conversation opens another door for expanding your brochure or new names for your contact list. Compare that to the debilitating feelings generated by the mathematical interviewing process.

Chapter 7

START WITH A HIT LIST

Your first step is to create a "hit list" of people you can call to say, "I'm thinking of starting my own business. Can we meet for coffee and get your thoughts?" The response rate for a coffee meeting is about 80% and you are almost always sitting with a decision-maker, not some human resources clerk who has already pre-judged you.

In addition, you can engage your family to help you build the hit list. Ask them to think of people in the neighborhood, your friends' parents, folks at church or synagogue, family friends and people from the baseball team to the dance class. Instead of isolating your family with the frustrations of sending resumes you can give them an active role in helping you build a network of people to contact.

Engage your family in developing the Hit List.

Ask your spouse and kids to think of people to add to the list.

Your hit list should include names, contact information and how you know them. You should be able to create a list of 50 people and continue to add to the list as you begin to contact people on your list. The Hit List is a serious first step that will help you feel in control of your future and create real momentum for sharing your brochure.

Chapter 8

THE BROCHURE SECRET

The brochure is designed to <u>never be published</u>. It should be a work-in-progress draft that you are going to show people to share your areas of expertise and get their thoughts.

The brochure is an effective mechanism to get in front of decision-makers and people who can refer you to decision-makers. It is simply a way to beat the mathematical odds of a job search.

You may be saying, "I have no intentions of going into business for myself. I need the security of a regular full-time job."

STOP!! You can both search for a job and test the waters of going into business for yourself. You make no commitment until an actual opportunity is brought to the surface. If someone asks you to propose a consulting agreement, you write a short proposal. If they indicate they would only consider employing someone with your skills, reach into your briefcase for a copy of your resume and know that you have beaten the mathematical odds.

The Brochure Strategy gets you in front of decision-makers to explore both consulting and employment possibilities.

Chapter 9

THE OUTSIDE THREE PANELS

You are going to design a three-fold pamphlet. On your computer, turn the paper to "landscape" and use a text box for each of the vertical pages.

The cover page should have your company name and a tag line. The tag line should be one or two sentences that reflect your leadership philosophy, short vision statement or a favorite quote.

➔ A friend with a financial background chose the phrase, "Calculating for the Good of Humanity."

➔ A colleague with a desire to be a leadership consultant wrote, "Leadership is like the flame on a candle. It can illuminate unlimited other candles without diminishing the original flame."

➔ A very practical individual simply stated, "Strategies for Success."

The first flap is a biography about three paragraphs. Don't copy your resume but write what you would have as an introduction if you were giving a keynote speech.

The back flap is for testimonials from people who would be impressive to have on your brochure because of their title or company name. You may wish to ask some of the people you meet for a one-line testimonial.

Example of the Outside three panels

Biography	Testimonials	
Bruce Matza's expertise is in strategic planning, executive mentoring, and building customer centric cultures.	Bruce had a profound impact on our business. CEO, Fortune 500	*BRM Enterprises*
His clients range from retail, healthcare, Realtor Associations, Senior Living to small family businesses.	We have a new future direction after Bruce facilitated a strategic planning retreat. President, Non-Profit	
Bruce has authored several publications and appeared on the NBC Today Show.	He has served as an adviser for over 20 years. Association Executive	*Our mission is to maximize the value of people. Your Staff and your Customers.*
	My Contact Info	

Chapter 10

THE INSIDE THREE PANELS

On the inside three panels you will want to list three major areas of expertise you bring to a company. I had to post all of my different skills and experiences on cards on the wall and keep regrouping them until I had the major categories of my expertise.

Once you have the major categories, there may be more than three. I actually had seven major categories but chose the three most relevant before each meeting with a decision maker.

Each of the internal pages of the brochure is labeled with one of your three categories. You then want to add bullet point examples that support each of the major categories. Try to provide concise descriptions of work you have done, showing quantifiable outcomes whenever possible.

Remember, the categories may change with each brochure depending on who you are meeting. A not-for-profit organization may be more attracted to fund-raising or program development, where a profit company may like to see more ideas on customer service or bottom line profitability.

Example of the Inside Three Panels

Strategic Planning	Customer Centric Culture	Executive Mentoring
Board and Senior Leadership Retreats with measurable and actionable outcomes.	Customer Centric clients include Fortune 500 companies, Non-profits, Charitable organizations, Small businesses, and local governments.	Leadership coaching to achieve strategic initiatives.
1-3-year plans with annual updates.	The Customer experience starts with senior leadership and impacts every aspect of your organization culture.	Mentored over 400 physicians with relationship challenges.
Advisory services for a year at no additional expense.		CEOs and Presidents represent over half of the executives being mentored.

Chapter II

HERE IS WHAT HAPPENS

A vast majority of people you call are willing to meet with you because you are asking for nothing but their advice. People like giving advice.

Your brochure should be a work-in-progress. The bottom line is that you do NOT want the brochure to look too finalized. You want to present it to the person you are networking with and allow them to critique it, make suggestions and write their suggestions on it.

The Brochure Strategy not only allows you to present all of your relevant skills, but you also control the conversation. You're not being interviewed and waiting for those few opportunities to share a skill or experience.

One response you may receive is that the brochure reminds them about something else you did in the past. You agree to add it to the brochure.

A critical part of your networking conversation is to ask who they know that may need your skills and service. This most often results in a referral to someone at the decision-making level.

You get to present all of your skills and experiences as well as control the conversation.

Another possibility is that they see something on the brochure and ask you what it would cost for you to consult with them on that project. You may wish to ask for the opportunity to come in and meet with their people in order to present a formal proposal. See the section on "Writing a Proposal" later in this book.

Possibly they see something on the brochure and tell you about someone who has recently expressed that specific need. This becomes a more specific referral where you may get a high-level introduction.

The final alternative is that they like what they see on the brochure and start talking to you about being employed with their company. You reach into your briefcase where you just happen to have a copy of your dynamite resume.

Chapter 12

WRITING A CONSULTING PROPOSAL

Your networking may result in being asked to propose your services on a specific project. Even if you are seeking an employment opportunity, it is always easier to find a job when you already have one. A project is real work and can provide an opportunity to get up, get dressed and visit your client while still networking for employment.

Here are some essential elements when writing a proposal:

Proposed Scope of Work – What is the exact defined parameters of the project? Who will you be working with from your client organization? How will the work be measured and how will you be accountable? What research or background information will be necessary to successfully complete the work?

Defined Outcomes – You need to agree with your client what you're trying to accomplish and state those goals as defined outcomes to the project. If possible, include measurable achievements. This gives your proposal credibility and often secures additional assignments.

Timeline of Services – It is critical that you properly allocate your time, especially if you have several projects

happening at the same time. It is always a good idea to overestimate the time it will take to complete an assignment and bring it in under your estimate. You also need to know the available resources of others you rely upon to compete the project.

Costs and Expenses – Lawyers and accountants can bill by the hour, but it was always to my advantage to bill by the project, especially a project over several months. Calculate a fair fee for the entire project and ask to be paid in increments at the end of each month the project is in process.

During that time, if other projects are identified, agree to continue the same monthly fee. In this manner, you can often develop a retained relationship. Your client should be willing to pay your monthly fee as well as incurred expenses.

Always add reimbursement for expenses that you will incur.

Chapter 13

GENE'S STORY

Bruce and I worked together in a retail organization where I managed the distribution and transportation activities that brought merchandise into the inventory and moved it around to our stores across the country. The distribution and transportation function are a costly part of the operations of any retail business and I was fortunate to have developed many of the necessary skills of understanding the negotiation of contracts to the management of a fleet of trucks.

I came from the "other side of the negotiation table" having been in transportation and freight handling methodology. We implemented best-in-class solutions to improve service to our stores, while generating tremendous cost savings.

Upon being downsized, I connected with Bruce and quickly saw the value of the brochure strategy that he shared with me. Back then the "resume blitz" was busy work, and very discouraging. The brochure strategy gave me the confidence of going into business for myself and I quickly designed a brochure and began meeting with executives of local businesses to show them how I could

save them major expenses in their overall supply chain costs.

I was never in the market for a job. I used the brochure to start a consulting business and quickly had several proposals accepted. Along the way, I found myself talking to a large Christian products retailer. It began as a consultation and eventually led to a position as Vice President of Supply Chain Management. My contract allowed me to assist on minor projects on my personal time, which allowed me to keep "irons in the fire." I enjoyed that job for seven years before deciding I again wanted to dust off the brochure strategy and build my consulting business.

One of the great things about the Brochure Strategy is that it honors people and opens doors. People are complimented to be asked to advise you on a new business venture and are very willing to meet and share their ideas. People feel compelled to refer you to other opportunities or bring you into their organization for a specific project.

Ultimately, the Brochure Strategy led to my own consulting business, managing the full-service supply chain activities for small to medium size companies. We specialize in managing transportation costs, right-sizing fleet operations, and licensing and customizing a Transportation Management System that is used by dozens of companies.

At our peak, we employed up to ten agents and our centralized support staff. Most recently I have brought in my grandson to learn the principals of our Brochure Strategy and to learn the business.

It is amazing to have started with a rough three-fold pamphlet and end up with a business that has protected my future and is grooming the next generation of my family.

Chapter 14

SUSAN'S STORY

I was very distressed to be downsized in my early fifties and the thought of having to compete with younger generations of workers to get back in the workforce.

When Bruce invited me to lunch and introduced me to the Brochure Strategy, I felt like he was offering me charity. I had no intention of going into business for myself. I needed to be back in the corporate world with people, a paycheck and benefits. My response to the Brochure Strategy was that it simply didn't apply to me. Bruce played tough love and put a pencil in my hand. "Just identify your three best skills that you can offer an organization. Forget about starting your own business. Use it to sharpen your interview skills in knowing what attributes you want to share about yourself,"

So, I reluctantly agreed to use the brochure to better identify the areas of expertise that I could offer an organization and some of the examples of accomplishments that would be helpful to articulate in an interview.

I found myself completing the brochure, more as a class project than a career search strategy. Afterall, Bruce

would want to see something when we met a week later, and he was still buying my lunch.

Then something happened! I was suddenly using the inside three panels to describe my career ambitions and my perfect next job to other people.

It was at a Chamber of Commerce meeting that I was sharing my brochure almost verbatim with an executive from an industry totally different than my past experiences.

Suddenly, he handed me his business card and asked if I would visit his office the next day. I was hired as his Director of Marketing a month later.

Chapter 15

NORMAN'S STORY

I have a retail background as Director of Accounting. Bruce and I were both downsized about the same time and began meeting over coffee to mentor each other. Both of us had twenty years in corporate life. Our discussion turned to brainstorming who we could contact in the retailing world, and how to develop a resume and great cover letter.

Bruce asked me to design a simple three-fold brochure to show my areas of expertise. At our next meeting, we were reviewing my very rough three-fold when Bruce asked about a single example buried in one of the categories under Accounting Skills titled "Auditing Vendor Contracts." We agreed that should be a major category because of the potential revenues and the fact that few retail organizations spend much time reviewing past vendor negotiated contracts.

To my amazement, almost every retail executive who reviewed my brochure zeroed in on that category. I was quickly managing several consulting assignments as a specialist in finding and collecting vendor commitments for advertising money, promotional support, merchandise

samples and markdown money. Pricing my services was easy as I offered a 50/50 split of all recovered revenues.

Five years later, I had three people working for me and a reputation throughout the retail industry for my expertise in recovering revenues from vendor negotiated contracts.

Chapter 16

CONCLUDING THOUGHTS

Bottom line, regardless of your desire to consult or be employed, the Brochure Strategy beats the mathematics of the resume game.

You beat the mathematics of the resume game.

The Brochure Strategy gets you in front of far more decision-makers to present your total capacity to add value to that organization as an employee or a consultant.

You control the direction of the meeting with decision makers.

It is easier, more creative, and far less depressing than sending out resumes and waiting for the phone to ring.

The brochure also helps you formulate your value to a prospective company that serves you well from both a consulting and employment point of view.

It is a motivating experience because you are not waiting for the phone to ring. You control the direction of your career.

You now have all the knowledge and power of the Brochure Strategy. Have a terrific time planning your next career and the rest of your life!

Send inquiries and success stories to Bruce at the following address:

Bruce R. Matza, Principal
INNOVATIONS in MANAGEMENT
3201 Countryside Court – Unit B
Woodbury, Minnesota 55129
651-337-2543